ALPHA for Seniors Guide

Alpha

Published in North America by Alpha North America, 2275 Half Day Road, Suite 185, Deerfield, IL 60015

© 2010 Alpha North America

Alpha for Seniors Guide

First printed by Alpha North America in 2010

Printed in the United States of America

ISBN 978-1-934564-47-9

1 2 3 4 5 6 7 8 9 10 Printing/Year 14 13 12 11 10

Contents

"Alpha for Seniors" Introduction

Given the demographic development in the United States, more and more individuals will be entering into the third stage of their lives, what we call "Senior Citizens". Of the 307 million people living in the U.S., 76 million belong to the so-called "baby-boomer" generation, those born between 1946 and 1964. Many of the early "Boomers" are now approaching their mid 60s. Today, 12.8% of Americans, or 39.5 million, are 65 years of age or older. By 2030 nearly 20% of Americans will be 65 or older. Many of our seniors don't have a personal relationship with Jesus and they will soon face an eternity separated from God. What can we do about this?

Seniors in America are among the most under evangelized groups in America. Why is this? One reason is because many in the church believe that if you don't reach an individual by early adulthood, you won't ever reach them for Christ. If we are really honest, then we must admit that many of our churches cater to the young and neglect the elderly. This is a trend that is not limited to our churches specifically but our society in general. Our society is "youth oriented" and the elderly have become disenfranchised at a time in their lives when they often need more focus and attention. In a sense, we have "warehoused" our elderly and studies show that more than 70% of nursing home residents receive less than one visitor per week.

Many nursing homes and assisted living facilities have little or very sporadic spiritual care. Today's pastors are often too busy to provide any services to these facilities. The majority of nursing homes and assisted living communities have no in-house spiritual care staff. To make the "spiritual gap" even larger, many seniors can't find the necessary transportation to get them to a local church on Sunday.

Now that we've painted a rather bleak picture of the spiritual wellbeing of our seniors let us explain the opportunities that are available for those Christians who reach out to this group of individuals. Many seniors have never heard that it is possible to have a personal relationship with Christ; this was never taught to them. Most don't understand who the Holy Spirit is or that they can receive power, peace and love by being filled with the Holy Spirit. We can safely say that most don't realize what a blessing they could be to their churches and communities if they would become prayer warriors. Enter the Alpha for Seniors Course!

The mission and vision of "Alpha for Seniors" is to give

ALPHA for Seniors

every person in the US, who is living in a nursing home, assisted living community, independent living senior community, or attending an adult day care center, an opportunity to attend an Alpha course and hear the good news about Jesus Christ.

Alpha's aim is to help our seniors enter into a personal relationship with Jesus and for those who already have this personal relationship in Christ, to grow in their faith.

Having this relationship with our Lord and Savior Jesus Christ will be a real blessing to seniors as they advance in age, experience health issues, possible loneliness and in the end, face death.

In addition, we believe God has a purpose for older people to help with the extension of His Kingdom. In particular, to become a great source of prayer support as Alpha spreads across America.

What does God say about old age?

God seems to reserve some of his most positive help for those who are ageing. In the Bible, older people are not only treated positively with dignity and respect, but they are encouraged to play an active part in the life of the community while they can, and be lovingly cared for when they cannot.

The Old Testament has several encouraging verses to promote this premise. God, speaking through the prophet Isaiah says:

Isaiah 46:4 *"Even to your old age and grey hairs I am he. I am he who will sustain you. I have made you and I will carry you; I will sustain you and I will rescue you."*

Proverbs 16:31 *"Grey hair is a crown of splendor."*

Proverbs 20:29 **"***The glory of young men is their strength, gray hair the splendor of the old."*

The Psalms encourage older people to believe in themselves—that they're valuable as they age. And even when they feel helpless and hopeless, He will be there with his presence and his strength. He will not forget them. That is one of the messages Alpha can bring seniors as well.

Psalms 92:12-15 "The righteous will flourish like a palm tree, they will grow like a cedar of Lebanon; planted in the house of the Lord, they will flourish in the courts of our God. They will still bear fruit in old age, they will stay fresh and green, proclaiming 'The Lord is upright; he is my Rock, and there is no wickedness in him."

"Alpha for Seniors" Opportunities

In the US, studies on self esteem demonstrate the 60's – 70's to be the peak time for self–fulfillment as people are free to be themselves and to pursue their chosen interests not necessarily for selfish ends. They often have reasonable health and economic stability. This stage can last well into the 80's but can suddenly and surprisingly come to an end as a result of severe health deterioration or a key bereavement.

It is interesting that during the last 20 years of our life, we have as many adjustments to make and new things to learn as in the first 20 years. This may include:

- adapting to changes in our health, physical ability and loss of social status
- dealing with emotions associated with loss and regret
- reduced energy/motivation to keep us occupied and involved with other people despite the changes in our personal circumstances
- coming to terms with our new surroundings and a new lifestyle

All these changes can be challenging for people with a strong faith. How much more challenging for those who do not believe in Jesus Christ!

STARTING AN ALPHA COURSE

Before you start running an Alpha course in a senior center, you will need to conduct some due diligence. Here are some points to consider:

- Most senior care centers or independent senior living communities have a diverse population of religious affiliations. Because of this, we recommend that you stay with the original Alpha DVDs as they work well in all settings.
- Is the senior facility cared

for by a chaplain or pastor? If yes, you will want to meet with him/her to discuss running the Alpha course and obtain their agreement and support.

- Does your church have a relationship with any senior facilities? If so, this might be a natural link for starting an Alpha course. You might also be able to recruit Alpha leaders from this pool of church members.
- Inform your pastor/priest about your intentions to running the Alpha course at a specific senior center.
- If you are approaching a new care center, Alpha can be a great way to start the relationship with the residents and the staff. Establish a good relationship with the volunteer/ activities coordinator and received approval from the Administrator before beginning an Alpha course.
- Be aware that you may run into family members or friends of the seniors and even care-givers who won't think highly of the outreach that Alpha is conducting.

You will need to show grace and kindness and yes, even diplomacy toward these individuals. In the end some of these skeptics might become the biggest Alpha advocates.

For independent living communities, you may also want to research if the senior facility has any "snow birds" residents, as these individuals will change their place of residence at least two times per year.

COURSE LOGISTICS
Many guests will have physical challenges—like poor eyesight, which would make reading difficult. They may also be confined to a wheelchair or need to use a walker.

Others will be hard of hearing so a **good sound system is very important**. So there are a lot of things to think about when you start setting up your course and when you are actually running it.

- **The best time**: Work with the senior center staff to find the best time to run the course.

It is important to remember that we are guests in the care facility. Many have staff that are overwhelmed with current work loads and responsibilities, so it is important that we do all we can to avoid adding work to their day. Setting up special meal accommodations does that. What we have found that works best in the nursing home and assisted living setting is to have a snack after the video and before/during the group discussions. This works well, as most elderly enjoy coffee/juice and a bar/cookie at activities. Try to be as flexible as possible. Find out when the care center can accommodate you, and when the volunteers are available. Often, assisted living and independent living communities can make it work in the early evening which works well if your volunteers are still working.

- **Location**: Find a location that is large enough, that has good acoustics and lighting. (Options will be limited in most care centers, so work closely with the staff)

- **Your Team**: Put together your team and make sure they are trained in how to run the Alpha course. Team members should also be people who have a heart for the elderly and - if possible - team members should receive or have some basic training on ministering to and working with the elderly. Know how to deal with people suffering from dementia (Alzheimer's and Parkinson's) and/or who may not be responsive. Here again, love, patience and perseverance are required. Input from the staff on specific physical limitations can be invaluable. Consider recruiting Christian staff members of the senior care facility.
- **Poor eyesight**: Alpha print resources are available in large font and can be ordered

on-line at the Alpha Store www.alpharesources.org.

- **Hearing impaired**: Course leaders should be aware of the fact that many course participants may have difficulty hearing. Besides holding the course in a quiet room, presenters and small group hosts should speak slowly and loudly. We also suggest turning on the closed-caption feature when viewing the presentation via the Alpha DVD. Those with hearing impairment could be encouraged to sit in the front row.

- **Weekend retreat**: During the Alpha weekend (often called "The Holy Spirit Weekend")

which usually happens around week 6 or 7 of the course, there are three talks that cover the person of the Holy Spirit. Given the amount of material that is covered and the physical capabilities of the participants, we would suggest using both Saturday and Sunday to complete this topic. In most Alpha courses the weekend would be held at a different location so that course participants could experience a retreat atmosphere. However, our recommendation is to hold the senior's weekend at the senior facility. There are a multitude of reasons for this, including the logistical issues, liability and again the limitations of the residents. Be creative in finding ways to make this part of Alpha special. One example that

was given to us was to bring in a youth group to serve lunch and fellowship with the residents on Saturday. The young people and the seniors can talk, sing songs together and play games (such as bingo). Again, flexibility is a key. In some assisted living and most independent living situations it may work to hold the "weekend" off-site depending on the capabilities of class members. The rule-of-thumb should be that if an off-site retreat excluded even one member from attending, you should stay on-site.

- **Praise and worship**: Praise and worship music should be incorporated into the Alpha course starting no later than week three. If you have a local musician that can play 2-3 songs before you start the course that would be an added plus. Otherwise, bring a CD recording and hand out song sheets. Familiar hymns might be a good starting point this example of familiar hymns might be a good starting point:

  – Great Is Thy Faithfulness
  – Amazing Grace
  – In the Garden
  – The Old Rugged Cross
  – Blessed Assurance
  – It Is Well with My Soul
  – Joyful, Joyful, We Adore Thee
  – Oh, for a Thousand Tongues to Sing
  – Christ the Lord Is Risen Today
  – Onward Christian Soldiers
  – And Can It Be, That I Should Gain
  – Praise to the Lord, the Almighty

- **Budget**: The Alpha course is free to the participants. As the food would typically be provided for by the senior facility, the cost of running an Alpha course for seniors should be minimal. Talk to your church to see if they would be able to cover the cost of the course manuals.

- **Free Bibles**: Have large print Bibles available for participants who might request one.

The Alpha leaders and helpers facilitating in the Alpha course play an important role in the Alpha course process. Alpha feels that it is important that these individuals have a love for the Lord and a heart to serve; in this case, a heart to serve seniors. At a minimum we suggest that all leaders and helpers should have attended an Alpha course and received leaders training. It would be great to get young adults and individuals with family members living in care centers involved in the Alpha course.

TYPICAL ALPHA COURSE: AGENDA

It is important to remain very flexible when it comes to schedules for Alpha for Seniors in a care center or assisted living community. Many factors can play a role. From an agenda standpoint, the basics remain for the most part; just abbreviated. A sample agenda for a nursing home may look like this:

9:30 A.M.	Alpha team meets to pray for course, set up AV equip, greet/gather guests
10:00 A.M.	Welcome by course leader: Alpha joke
10:10 A.M.	Presentation (DVD or live talk)* (time allowed depends on which video used)
10:40 A.M.	Break for coffee/snack and form small groups for discussion
10:50 A.M.	Small group discussion (length depends on physical capability of guests)
11:10 A.M.	End

Again, base your times on capability of the guests and what works with the schedule of the care center staff. In an independent living community, you may be able to lengthen these times closer to a standard alpha schedule at church. (depending on the meal/snack situation) Remember, there can easily be 80 and 90 year old residents in these communities too, so remain flexible.

*To reduce the time required for the talk, the "Express" DVD could be used in senior care facilities. Our experience is that residents have limited strength and attention capabilities in the nursing homes especially. For this reason, we recommend the "Express" version. The entire program should last about an hour in a nursing home. In an assisted living community you may be able to use the

full-length videos. We usually try to limit the program to an hour and forty-five minutes for assisted living. It is just too tiring for most residents to go longer than this (these times do not include the Alpha team set up and prayer time).

"Alpha for Seniors" Group Discussion

As stated earlier, it is imperative that all Alpha leaders participate in an Alpha course prior to leading one. Alpha leaders must also first receive small group training. Group discussions may be difficult as guests offer unique challenges such as difficultly with hearing, speech and reading. As is common in Alpha small groups, some participants might be very opinionated and not open to other points-of-view. There might also be a senior in a group that just doesn't get along with one of the other residents. We recommend that before starting the course the course administrator should discuss these issues with the senior center staff to be made aware of individuals who don't get along with each other. This should be taken into consideration when forming the small groups.

Getting guests to talk about themselves is a good way of encouraging discussion. They all have stories to tell, and the fact you're prepared to listen to them and that you value what they say, is so important. Job 12:12 *"Is not wisdom found among the aged?"* We have to be careful not to patronize them but to give them enough time to express themselves.

How can we be effective in ministering to older people?

Dealing with the elderly can be different from interacting with your colleague at work. The better you understand seniors, their needs, their thinking and how to communicate with them, the easier it will be to present the Gospel to them. Here are some tips that will improve your experience and lead to a successful Alpha course:

- Pray daily for the Alpha course and each participant by name. Ask God to give you wisdom and patience when running the course.
- Pray as you go into a care facility and pray as you leave, that your team would be protected from any negative spiritual attacks.
- Listen to what the seniors have to say, because they have a wealth of knowledge and experience that they are willing to share. Listen, listen, listen.
- Respond to their questions with sensitivity.
- Be yourself – take off the mask
- Find young people who have a heart for the elderly and get them involved in running the course. Seniors love to interact with young people.
- Acknowledge the presence and role of the Holy Spirit and ask that he fill you and your guests anew every day.
- Treat each guest as if they were super special and

deserve your full attention.
• Treat the staff at the senior facility as if they were super special.

• If possible and available, have your team go through basic training for ministering to the elderly.

"Alpha for Seniors" Checklist

The following is helpful information that you may consider before beginning an "Alpha for Seniors" course:

- ✔ Enquire with your church if they are supporting any senior centers
- ✔ Inform your senior pastor of your intentions to run an Alpha course
- ✔ Review list of senior care facilities in your area
- ✔ Create excitement about the "Alpha for Seniors" course in your church
- ✔ Select and train your Alpha leaders & helpers
- ✔ Establish contact with facility administrators & staff
- ✔ Alpha senior resources (course manual & leaders guide available in large print, Alpha DVD with "Alpha Express" & closed-caption feature)
- ✔ Register your "Alpha for Seniors" course on Alpha USA website (alphausa. org, under running a course)
- ✔ Understand senior's physical constraints—poor eyesight, hearing, mobility, dementia (Alzheimer's & Parkinson's) and how to deal with these issues
- ✔ Organize room assignments at location
- ✔ Determine Alpha start date, number of sessions & time of day offered
- ✔ Coordinate Alpha meal or snack, if not already provided by senior care facility
- ✔ Schedule weekend retreat dates
- ✔ Remember the basics: use large print for all reading material, use subtitles on DVD and adjust volume accordingly, speak one at a time with a clear, slow and audible voice
- ✔ Remember that prayer and preparation are the under-gird for everything we do
- ✔ Contact Alpha USA with any needs, questions or concerns on the "Alpha for Senior" ministry

Next Steps

After completion of the Alpha Course participants will inquire about next steps, especially those who have had a life-conversion on the course. There are three main things that we recommend post Alpha Course:
- Prayer
- Reading the Bible
- Small group study and fellowship

Prayer is our way to communicate with our heavenly Father and we should all do this daily. Prayer should be done individually and also in community. There are many resources available on prayer and we suggest that the course leaders not only emphasize the importance of prayer but help the participants establish a good prayer life.

Studying and meditating on God's word is also important as course participants continue on their spiritual journey. All participants should own or receive a Bible (large print) upon completion of the course. Encourage the participants to spend a few minutes each day reading the Bible, meditating on God's word and asking that the Holy Spirit guide them during this important study. Many people like to journal their thoughts during and after their Bible study, so please also recommend this.

After experiencing the Alpha Course participants ask if it is possible to continue learning about and experiencing God in the small group setting. We encourage this and Alpha has some course material that can be used for this purpose. We suggest that you visit the Alpha website www.alpha.org and review the follow-up and small group resources in the Alpha "Store". We highly recommend the nine-session course "A Life Worth Living" which is based on the book of Philippians.

If the team could continue to meet with the residents following the Alpha course this would be great . . . especially if you have someone who accepts Jesus for the first time. If this is not possible for a team member, try to find someone in your church body that would be willing to come along side this new Christian for nurturing and growth.

In closing, we would like to mention that Alpha is a Christian non-profit organization and our Kingdom work depends fully on the financial support that we receive from donations. The Alpha Course is free to the participants and any request that might be made for financial support is done ever-so-gently. This "ask" typically comes in the end-of-course questionnaire when participants are asked if they want to help out in one of the following areas:

- Hospitality/greeter
- Food/table setup
- Prayer team
- Financially supporting the Alpha ministry

Please be aware that in nursing homes and assisted living communities, most of the residents are considered "vulnerable adults" and are protected by law. Asking them to contribute is not allowed. There are some people who may not be in this status, but it is best not to solicit anything but prayer support from them.

Independent living communities are different. In most instances, giving these individuals an opportunity to support your Alpha financially would be appropriate. If a course participant indicates that they would like to help the Alpha ministry financially, we recommend that you give them a copy of our donations brochure or ask them to contact us at the telephone number listed below.

One final note: please share with us any experiences that you have had running an Alpha course for seniors. We would love to incorporate this into our booklet and share with others who have a heart for seniors.

Contact Information

For more information on "Alpha for Seniors" please contact:

Alpha U.S.A.
2275 Half Day Road
Suite 185
Deerfield, IL 60015
Tel: 800.362.5742
Tel: + 212.406.5269
e-mail: info@alphausa.org
www.alphausa.org

Alpha in the Caribbean
Holy Trinity Brompton
Brompton Road
London SW7 1JA UK
Tel: +44 (0) 845.644.7544
e-mail: americas@alpha.org
www.alpha.org

Alpha Canada
Suite #230 – 11331 Coppersmith Way
Riverside Business Park
Richmond, BC V7A 5J9
Tel: 800.743.0899
Fax: 604.271.6124
e-mail: office@alphacanada.org
www.alphacanada.org
To purchase resources in Canada:

David C. Cook Distribution Canada
P.O. Box 98, 55 Woodslee Avenue
Paris, ON N3L 3E5
Tel: 800.263.2664
Fax: 800.461.8575
e-mail: custserve@davidccook.ca
www.davidccook.ca